Sugar Factory glows with a gloriou[...] deep inside the language of listening and attention. An[...] material textures transmit in exclamatory abundance the a[...]ty [...] time past [...] Lines such as "your green stays green" and "how am I?/ to end this poem" beautifully capture an attempt to hold on to fleeting impermanence. The book delights in expectancy as it flows effortlessly from generation to generation, across continents, and makes a gift of embodiment to each of its varied speakers allowing for the ecstatic possibility to "leave one's body and return." Reading *Sugar Factory* one is struck simultaneously by the resilience and slippage of memory as it weaves in and out of fragmented storytelling while also asking: what is it that this telling gets done, what of memory's remains does one have to contend with, and what is it to speak towards someone who is no longer alive. As "This I" continues to shift and redefine itself, the reader soaks in the pleasure of being a ready recipient moving both towards specific familial pasts and a dreamlike unreality as each environment evoked leaves a trail of meditative intimacy.

ANNA GURTON-WACHTER

Like Whitman's "Song of Myself," Hughes's *Sugar Factory* is a laud for the land, a deep song of praise for the ecstasy in the ordinary. Riding the train, peeling fruit, contemplating streaks of color—here we find everyday encounters opening doorways to memory, both intimate and ancestral. The result is a quietly fierce collection of poems which spans coasts and continents as it boldly "carries the voices of the living/and the dead."

PATRICIA KILLELEA

These poems make me so glad. I don't think I've ever seen such a charming use of the exclamation point. And there is such a vastness to these little poems—the way Joanne Kyger or Larry Eigner were able to write like brushstrokes—Emily Wallis Hughes lives fully, sensually in the natural world, in the city, and in a family's past. You will feel so at home in these poems; they are a tonic.

MATTHEW ROHRER

Emily Wallis Hughes's poems are an absolute joy to read. As a fellow poet—and a fellow Californian—I greatly admire her keen ability to evoke a sense of place. She has that essential gift of making one feel totally immersed in the world of her poems—and of conjuring in the reader a sense of delicious and aching nostalgia for things not in the reader's experience. With its light touch and its exceptional range of techniques, voices, and registers, *Sugar Factory* is a treasure.

GEOFFREY NUTTER

SUGAR FACTORY

Emily Wallis Hughes

artwork by Sarah Riggs

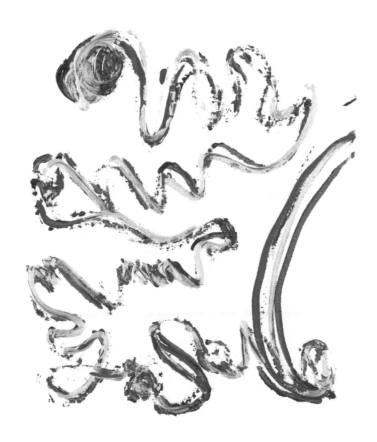

SPUYTEN DUYVIL
New York City

Library of Congress Cataloging-in-Publication Data

Names: Hughes, Emily Wallis, author. | Riggs, Sarah, 1971- artist.
Title: Sugar factory / Emily Wallis Hughes ; artwork by Sarah Riggs.
Description: New York City : Spuyten Duyvil, [2019]
Identifiers: LCCN 2018046559 | ISBN 9781947980952
Classification: LCC PS3608.U3578 A6 2019 | DDC 811/.6--dc23
LC record available at https://lccn.loc.gov/2018046559

Magnolia up the road is "unincorporated"

— Lisa Fishman

is there too much of the sky

— Larry Eigner

I chased after trees in another part of the world

I wanted to know their name their family

I bring you a damp fish

— Sarah Kirsch

CONTENTS

A Breeding Method

Oh I love their heated fingers

I love their amber minds

These very, very old women

Breeding ordinary shapes

Then handling them as delicate paper

These very, very old women

Breed a pasture in the shape of stone!

Breed a pasture in the shape of birds

Breed a pasture in the shape of corn!

I will gladly be a very, very old woman

I will breed a large glass

Or else

A tall jar

The more ordinary the better

Afternoon

I don't know if time   is

worth growing

                 the robins

            are here

in the currant trees

SEAMSTRESS

Antonie my grandmother was a seamstress in Germany

She came to America on a large ship

She lived in a boarding house in a tiny room

She sold her zither to a man who could not play it

Took care of children who were not her children

Bought a Brooklyn deli ran the deli with two other women

Met a man who was once a chimney sweep in Nuremberg

They married, they had children

Five children

Late at night she made clothes for them

A strawberry dress for my mother

A generous hem

Always generous hems always!

At school my mother couldn't see the chalkboard

In the one room schoolhouse

She needed glasses

Antonie said no you need to be like the other children

My mother pretended to see what she wanted to learn

Yes that's what she would tell me when we were inside

Of our house in the Sonoma Valley yes like how

She pretended to like the taste of powdered

Milk in the Pennsylvania winters

Day

purple vetch I am serious PURPLE VETCH

and the lupine all gathered and spooned out in bowls—

                                the lupine, alled!

                         where will we stay now, mother?

                    what did you eat?

I always ate the begonias

                           I still eat the begonias!

It's Clear

So clear here at Limantour Beach I can see the Farallones

You know, Mom makes art installations in the back

       yard now, with found objects

            There's one with a broken red wheelbarrow!

      A long stick leaning up against a redwood tree

     Several   turkey feathers stuck into

an old stump

            And I have to tell you!

             How he sat with me

                And how he watched the wind gather

                   my houndstooth

                      dress after two cigarettes, and how

                       significant I imagined it to be

                   As usual,

             Mom is doing yoga

           on a threadbare towel, I'm writing

              this poem to you

Let's eat raisins and chardonnay grapes

   at the same time

      WHY   I ask aloud

    are the fishing boats so close to the shore?

      Look at these eight

     sand dollars, completely intact! I want to give

         three, maybe four to you. Should I?

            put them in the raisin box for safe keeping

These flies   are they attracted to the drying seaweed or

  is that kelp? I will ask them what they know

Day

I left my aphrodisiac in Sinai

I'm pretty sure!

Occur

Autumnal Equinox. The earth revolves

around the sun. Its axis remains

tilted   23.5 degrees from the perpendicular

when the hemispheres face the sun   equally

I told you about it?

When   the equi-

noxes occur

the tilt of

the earth causes different latitudes

on earth   to receive varying amounts of sunlight

throughout the year

I went

to the exhibit,

I think

I told you about it   De Young

Took the Vallejo ferry   then the 44 bus   very nice

hopefully I won't be losing a tooth

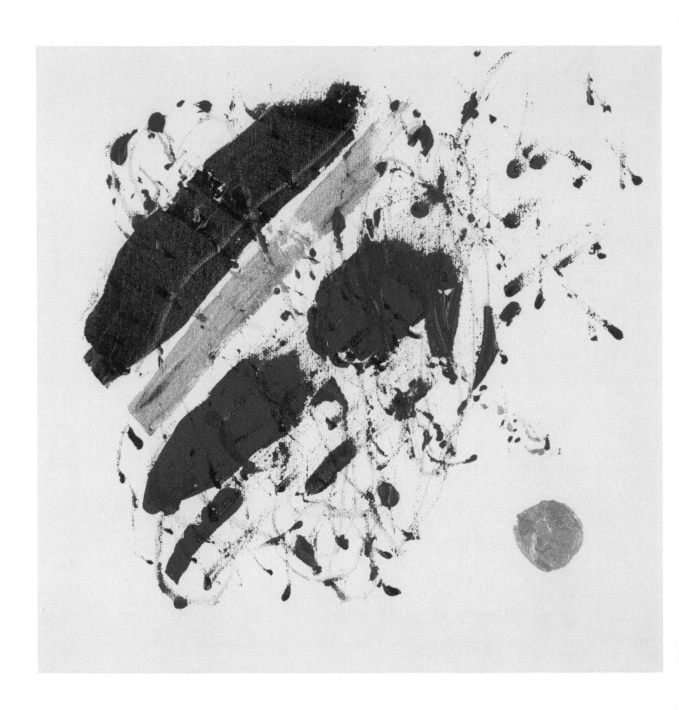

DEMETER DEMETER

Collect the poppies before 8:00 am!

        Learn from a man on his hands and knees

            Watch how he uses the paring knife, as half-

ghost, lingering on

Gentle pharmacists   I shall taper myself off to a mere spoonful a day, with anise

I am a ready woman

in the slow river   five days after

the petals have fallen

Demeter, Demeter   Demeter I am wanting

I am wanting

     family life

     and
young leaves!

Oh where is
     my little glass cup
where is my lock   of

Keats's hair?

DAY

She grew tired

She grew tired

She grew tired

She went out

in the meadow

not too far

away

to collect ladybugs in the blue flax

sing by the creek

sing with the ladybugs here, by the creek

She starts making a basket out of Yerba Buena and out of her own hair

and her sister's hair and out of out of dog blood and out of

the elderberries dropped on the gravel path to her best friend's house

She, she forgets

I forget how

HYDROCHLORIDE FOREST TREATMENT

yes   you can believe

I have eaten the sterling silver

hello   small number of children

       I am one of the many who are prone to walk   looking for the animals I once knew

shall we feed in the meadow   together?

thank you for calling the FDA

hello? who is the one who has lost all sense of other considerations?

I am pregnant with the colorful rings around the lights!

the sequence of straight blue lines should be considered

the hands of your doctors should be considered

the sequence of straight blue lines should be considered

the hands of your doctors should be considered

the sequence of straight blue lines should be considered

the hands of your doctors should be considered

I am pregnant with the colorful rings around the lights!

in the eye   and in the angle-closing part of the body

I feel a certain action

                    the full breath of a maximum dose

the voices of the coma! come out in the garden

where I have awoken with the cinnamon

basil

I see you!

small number of children

I see you

DAY

The tulips don't care that the people make fun of them

Because they're orange

My mother skips with me across the parking lot

We've just been to the library

It's a beautiful day!

We found our favorite tree

DAY

Nothing in the mail—

Sister

was sitting next to me

Mother always saw her

She's in my cheese and lettuce

sandwiches

She's in my Mother's

cursive

when she says goodbye to me

in a letter again

HYDROCHLORIDE FOREST TREATMENT

seasonal patients!

be sure to obtain the cartilage of the manufacturer

seasonal patients

your algae grows in the stomach

you will remain the same age as your information

                                          I befriend

the waters of Arcata

Planting the Phlox

Opa liked to look at the flowers while sitting on the porch as he smoked

    Their petals   reddened pink Pollen   orange as the kitchen linoleum

He was retired now   he remembered again

No more waiting tables in Manhattan

No more sleeping in that room he rented

What he and his wife had now

a wide field   a vegetable garden   a fence

a house with an attic—the attic filled

with children's clothes made by his wife

the old outhouse, there from the year before he could

    afford plumbing

old cars, no longer workable

some furniture   a color television   the road   that road—his daughter nearly killed

on that damn road   dogs and cats killed too

He knows

he will die before getting to the hospital

He knows that is now a

trivial matter

DAY

Sister pours Lipton tea for my doll

She braids my hair as I watch

                              the oak tree

She sets a typewriter on the living room floor

She arranges

mallard tail feathers

on my nightstand

                                                  Sister, I know you favor

                                                    the dark!

blue embroidery thread

DAY

The priest was wrong.

DAY

The nuns were right.

After Talking with Sappho

all of the tiles are pink though not

too pink

in your handwritten letter

also pink

the egrets are very still

above the cooling pies

a modest brunch is underway

in the adjoining room

from my window I admire

groves of men

DAY

Went to that   jewelry store on Fifth Avenue   early '60s

take a photo of blue chair

take a photo fancy black table

take a photo carpet clean

           I want to be drab,

               sage   turtleneck

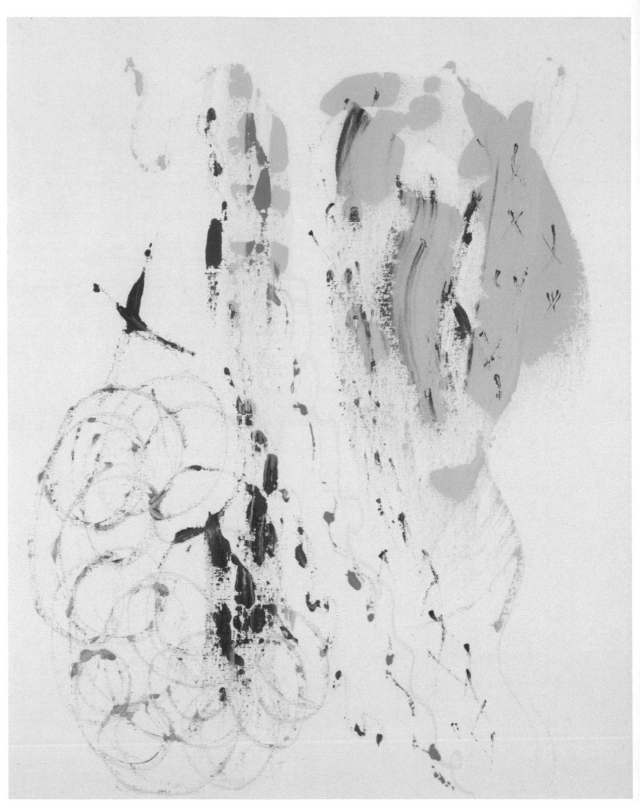

Day

In the tulles I held the pot

I made soup

out of the rosary beads

grandmother gave me

pressed by Carmelite nuns

their rose petals ground into a fine peach

powder

Here,

take my sieve!

You can keep it

LOVE LETTER

It's the little white house on the right

Read that poplar tree poem

This is just one of those things! we

just have to live with

Woman

Why do you dream of Poland

I think of you as St. Margaret. Why are you

swimming across the Rhine to France

You've changed your name

just like Sarah Kirsch

Why do you want to work in the sugar

factory, right next to her

DAY

the chives I want

how masculine

bound

This I

Children in the very

tiny orchard

who throw peach pits over the fence

There! For the bobcats

There! For the sheep!

This I, now in

the long-dead nectarine

tree

wrapped in chicken wire

My Love!

A flock

of bronze

quail

Michaux my

crushed seeds

      They

please will and may see you now,

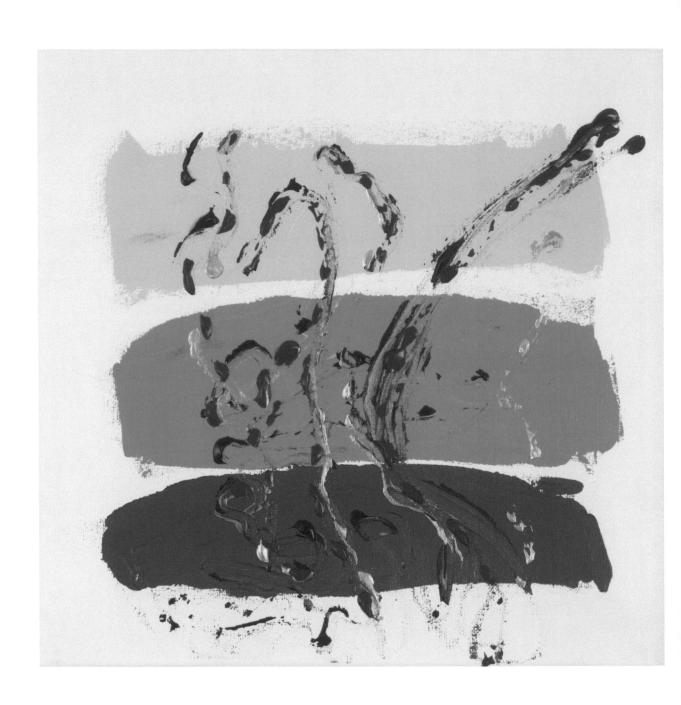

THE SKY

It always seems to be properly assembled

even when it's lost its diaphragm

Too many predictions!

The air, pressing all acute

Still, though, the sky

is a good idea

*

Mosquitoes

around the almost-

(how does one say)

mother-in-law

grating nutmeg into her

oatmeal

Did you see my knitting?

My herring?

*

A woman doing her cross-
stitching
on the subway her
violet!
wool violet coat

*

There are two
cows coveting my
favorite pink coffee
cup I think
I will wait and see
what they choose to do

DAY

there's no need to wash it off

see how the soil shows you

what? you were

marjoram,

so tender

your green stays green

Day

cluck cluck say the fans

cluck cluck!

cluck cluck say all of the library books

I cannot say when asked

what was

the distraction

Your rhythm will delete all of your past

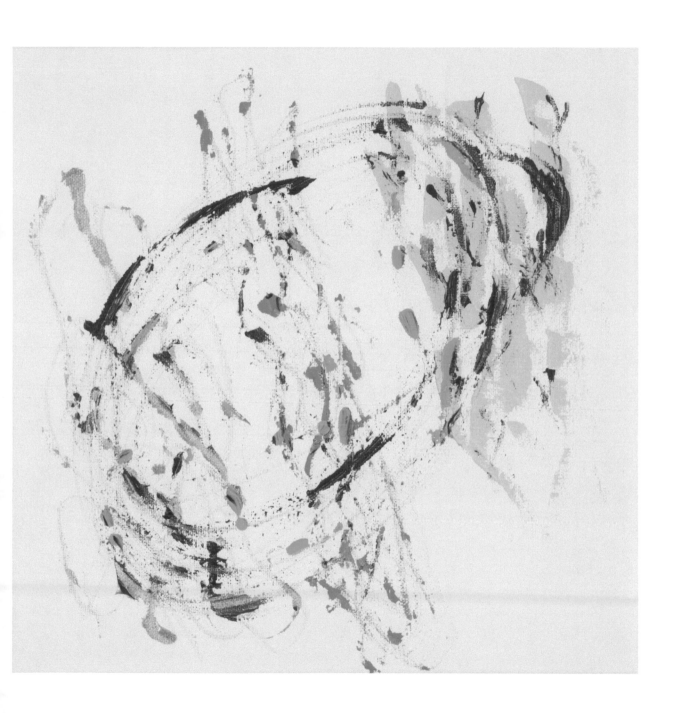

Day

I did not Instagram a photo of Mexican farmworkers picking strawberries in Salinas

The trees were here long before all of our given names

A monarch pin on his lapel. I said
to him, you

have a monarch!
It looks real on you
Just

 past the Smart and Final

a yellow warning sign reads "Drifting Sand"

DEAR JOY

you are an anklet

of gold alkali flies

you may stay

YET ANOTHER DREAM OF THE OLD HOUSE IN PENNSYLVANIA

There are grandmother-embroidered bluebirds

on the pillow left in what's left of the house

go find the bluebirds in the hidden closet

through the smallest door

You have the key to the passageway—

Yes, let's go there, to the passageway!

It does not lead anywhere but you've seen

in a bit of sun

how the princess pine

grows where it ends

You open the window to smoke a few cigarettes

and a couple more

just like the women before you

after dinner

Did you know?

The morning glories

open on our quilts

Yes   all day

A Warm Evening in June

my head rests

on his lap

we've just had poppy

rugelach and apricot

linzer cookies

oh and the '40s

jazz and the wind in the cork

oak's leaves

the birds of Davis are still

awake   he shows me

a photo of the ultramarine

speckled crow's egg

we saw a few days

before we walked under-

neath the coastal redwoods

from the windowsill I pick up

one of the small rocks he has

collected over many years

he makes

sky from these

No One is Here, Liliya

Teacher, tell me, who is raining?

I have a bowl Liliya I will

Let the rain fill it, pour it out

Liliya my student my dear one

Who has died? Tell me no

One is in our garden

No one is picking the tomatoes, cucumbers

No one is in the kitchen, making mamaliga for everyone

No one is writing on the table, the desks

No one is telling us how to eat the mamaliga

No one lives in the suburbs

No one is an immigrant no one

Is living in the suburbs! No one remembers how

To make the mamaliga

Tell me, do you see the bowl I

Remember it was wooden

If I find it in the grass Liliya

I will bring it to a place we will recognize

NOSTRAND AVENUE

red wine stain on a beige bra

HAHA!   the light says

on the pavement   bread

empty sugar packet

the hairdresser buys tangerine

peonies

hello, we are your children!

say all of the colors

Words Like Egypt

I am under the mind

I stay

seated on the couch by the window

drinking coffee, reading his texts

and poems with words like Egypt,

good, and robin eggs.

How am I?

to end this poem

without going outside, without

seeing people,

talking to someone.

Day

he took the white porcelain

bowl out of the cupboard he

placed it in the sink

he forgot what he was doing and walked into the other room

he remembered

he walked back into the kitchen

he ground some coffee

he looked at the bowl

in the sink he forgot what he was doing he walked into

the other room

he thought he walked

back into the kitchen he opened

the refrigerator took out a bag

of cherries he placed gently the bag

into the white porcelain

bowl he noticed the blue

rim of the bowl for the first time what

does one do now?

he asked aloud the cherries were still

in the bag

a clear plastic bag with holes I'm missing

a step he said he walked

into the other room

The Black Forest

Could I follow these worn cobblestones into the Black Forest?
Your Oma's brother is there.

Disabled, crippled they once said.
Degenerate they would call him.

Go into   the Black Forest.
Be lost   there forever.

Once you were called degenerate too, hidden
away in a bleached room, marked with
the letters of your odd affliction.

The letters are gone. You are not
as you once were, no —

Go into   the Black Forest.
Be lost   there forever.

You are happy among

the silver trees
of air—*hello,*
branch maidens?

You will find him. I know.
I've brought a blueberry pie.

HONEY

I feel so full

    Yes, I'll try honey in my coffee

I watched you pour it, stir, say: *there's a bit*

            of a jolt at first but I haven't gone back to sugar

        since I started

     I'm staying with it—you?

     I'm stayed, still, by this moonrise

      in a painting, the print of which

        you sent me. You wrote on its back, as you cried

        into the alkaline waters of Mono Lake

      It was summer, August, and I was with you then

     I was with you though you

were there only, fully in poetry

    with you I read

Joanne Kyger in the afternoon

     with you I slept, just

         north of Bolinas

      with you I drank the Manchurian

        alders planted by an old woman

      in the Mayacamas hills with

you, I bore

the heat of the day, as I

watched the grapes ripen on hot vines

with you I slept peacefully, soundly with you

with you! with the window opening to the East

so as to, therefore, be closer to the Mayacamas

with you I bend to them, oh

how I bow to them and to you

Lor—

ine, Lorine! Niedecker   I need you mother Lorine

Lorine Lorine!

I will carry you

I won't let anyone

forget you

You are the poem

I have given my time to all   of you

THREE WOMEN

The woman of unknown origins in Mainz

says I saw everything, everything.

It is true, she has seen everything, but her mother never heard her.

She speaks, says after loss

there is always beauty. Then

loss again

beauty again

loss ever

youth over   the daffodil

death under   the milkmaids.

This you can count on, she says, over

black tea and butter cookies.

To find her I make Alsatian Pear Kugel with Prunes.

To find her I follow the directions.

To find her I pre-heat the oven.

To find her I grease a 9-inch springform pan.

To find her I peel all of the pears, save one.

To find her I heat three tablespoons of oil in a cast-iron skillet.

To find her I sauté the onions.

To find her I soak the bread in warm water. I mix. I stir in. I pour the batter.

I make the sauce. Pears. Prunes. Cinnamon. Lemon juice.

The saved pear I finely grate, stir in.

I unmold from the pan, onto a serving platter, with

spooned sauce.

*

The German-Polish-Jewish woman in Brooklyn says I saw everything, everything.

She cannot speak of her mother who died from gangrene

she says to me, over apple juice

served in her dead sister's

martini glasses in her

rent-controlled apartment.

We both drink.

We press our backs into the chartreuse

couch cushions.

I type up her recipes, one by one.

To speak with her I make each recipe, one by one.

The apple cake speaks the most.

I combine two recipes for apple cake—one from her sister, one from her other sister.

Three Golden Delicious and three Granny Smith.

I do as she says.

I make the cinnamon sugar and set it aside.

I cream the oil and sugar, add the eggs, one at a time. I add the flour, baking powder, orange juice. I don't forget the vanilla.

I mix well.

I grease a large tube pan.

Carefully I eye the batter in order to make even layers.

I pour one third of the batter into the pan.

I arrange delicately, one third of the apples.

One third batter more. One third apples more.

One third batter more. One third apples more.

No, I do not forget to sprinkle the cinnamon and sugar on top, evenly.

Yes, I will oven at 350 degrees for one and a half hours until golden brown.

Not a minute more.

*

I saw everything, everything, I say to the plum tree in an old poet's backyard.

The Meyer lemon tree grins and says *ah no, you most certainly did not!*

The plum tree nods in agreement.

My dearest fruit trees you are right!

No longer a girl engaged to a boy, I set out to make my mother's plum jam.

The cat who lives in this house will be entertained.

It is my job, after all, to entertain this house and cat while the poet is away.

One cup of sugar for one cup of fruit.

Unless the fruit is sweet and ripe, mother always says.

I make sure to use some harder fruit—more pectin

that way.

I don't forget the lemon juice.

I add a bit of lemon zest too, because I feel like it.

I low boil, I assure my mother.

Yes, I am eating dinners.

The jam is thickening—sheeting it's called, mother says.

Oh yes, I have the jars boiled, and ready.

I say goodbye. I must pour now.

DAY

Two limpets

      take hold

in my palms

                I see an indigo

              sun drifting further

and further away

      from us

I wake

the limpets have left

leaving trails

on my fingertips

              Could you tell me

              where

they've gone?

I would like to follow

age

with them

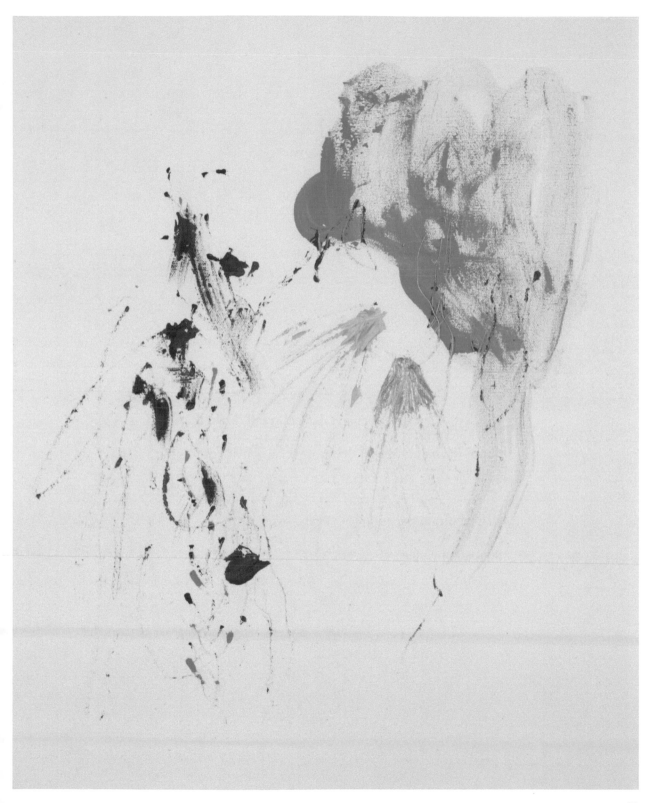

Waiting for Breakfast

It feels odd, to do nothing

with my hands. You tend the stove.

The kelp observes

the monotonous rocks. And the arctic

terns are in the alders, down

in the tidal flat, just as you

recalled. Can't say what anyone will recall down there,

but of the bark, here on the shore, I can say it continues

stripped from the cut trees. I'm so sorry

it's instant coffee.

Sarah Kirsch Walks Through Corona, Queens

there's a run in my stocking

sister called, said, *going*

is the only event   I'm

wearing my mother's old black shoes

you're wearing your old mother's old black shoes?

I don't mind

the concrete here

the tomatillo sauce tastes like water

(I'm   trying to explain the counterintuitive)

there's a run in my stocking

The Myelin

One gardenia on a woman's

table. 1929 we have Sauvignon

blanc.

Pinot. Grigio.

1933. 1938. Germany, she was friendly

with the ship captain.

Her papers!

They smelled of gardenias

The war bodies'

figure is gone

Its figure is

only color

only remains

And the gardenia is

upright. The gardenia —

was it ever real?

Does it matter? How it smelled?

Once it mattered. There's one

made of tissue paper

There's

one made

of grass. There's

one made of mud

and teeth

Uncles' teeth

There's one made of flour, of course

and brown sugar

And one made of marrow!

The marrow in the grass

grass in —

The marrow in the house

The marrow in the room

The marrow in the bird

The marrow left in the bird

The marrow in the acrobat's

myelin

The myelin in the acrobats

The myelin in the man in

the batman costume

What I mean:

I have to name the myelin

No what I mean

is that it can't yet be located

by you or me or anyone

What I mean is there

is myelin in

the marrow and

it will stay there

Yes! the marrow is in

the myelin

in the sandstone

in one of my feet

and yours

the myelin-marrow

came out of the bodies and it

has stayed out

encircling us

in red lakes

lakes in lakes

It goes into the trees

the buildings

the knives

It eats what we eat

It cuts the hair

It shaves

It has shaved

the crucifix on

the salmon wall

Stupendous, it says

just stupendous.

What did we do

when we named it

What was the guide?

The baby

What if we didn't

name the baby

Is that protest?

And then we are photographed

as art

Name the baby knee

Name the baby thigh the baby ankle to the

toe but not the brain

Not the amygdala

Not the church

Not the statue nor? the

saint

Not the legs

Not the sexual position not

the pants

Not the bottle of gingko leaves

This kind of thinking was a

three-limbed tree and

a poet's long, brown wavy hair

A brown spot on a dog

The wallpaper by the radiator

Peppermint wallpaper in the room

The twin bed over the mouth

A spot of blood on

the pillowcase

My mother is in the hospital

She hears woodpeckers

bluebirds

as she is in labor

Her mother is not there

Her sister is not there

I'm being videotaped as I

write this

She is in labor

There is no sky

Or what is left of the

sky is made of

hot porcelain

So much hot porcelain

The lights were on

It was a red building

Twenty stories high

*

Fire I want Fire

I want love next to this

aluminum coated stainless steel

The air was next to it

Glass was next to it

I wanted oil

Even the pepper was stayed

on it

The steel wool

The sponge

The Palmolive

I bring the pan into my bedroom

Throw it on my bed

Someone says

This is oil this is oil

This is blood

This is wood

You have to oil the wood

yearly, to keep it nice

Find a good oil to use like

walnut

I asked for the sun

through the clouds and

that's what I received

Outside there are green snakes

A girl in a white shirt and jeans

plays frisbee, smiles

She is standing next to

a page of the newspaper

on the grass

Where are you

last evening of 1938

Where are

you

infinite acrobats with dyed red hair

You lay on top of

a mother's crocheted blanket

or are you under it

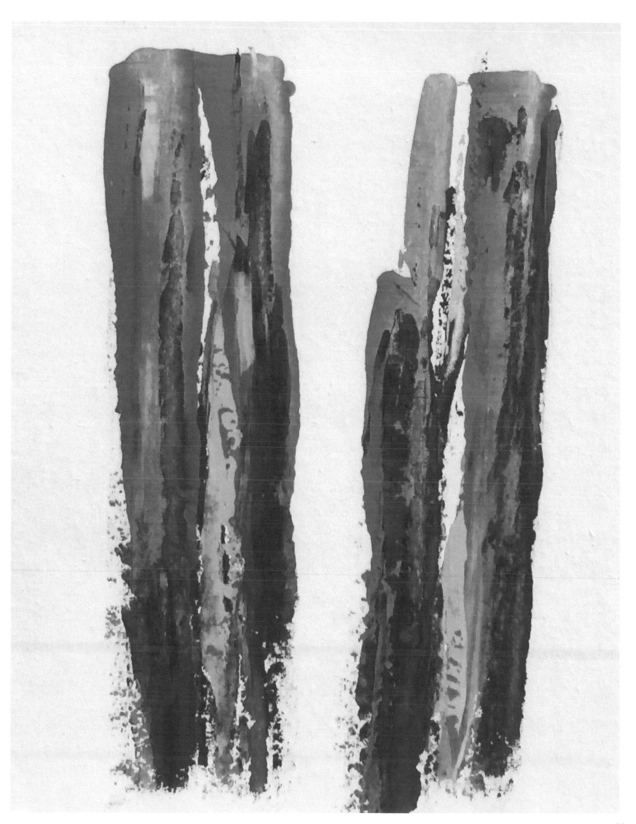

What Was Left

are you sitting down? this could be hard

rain falls in the Cabernet vineyard

a constant rain

there is no wind

there is solstice

and there is lunch

*

I am these six tiny buttercream pointsettas on the Scandinavian princess cake

I have learned it is possible!

to leave one's body and return

*

summer solstice

I'll come back into my body for awhile

there is a table in it, and on top of the table: mortadella,

olives, cheese, and a sliced baguette

there's enough for everyone

mother and I

share shot-

glasses of Chartreuse

she tells me what it's like to give birth

*

I know the nice family of gray foxes

they have invited me over for tea

mother too

YOU AND I

who is speaking

the two of us   and

only only   *we*

listen to the clarinet

play to the oboe from within

our kitchen cupboards

we don't open them!

there isn't any need —

our throats have kept the amaretto

in our one very tall

frosted glass

Day

The sun imagery traces its own development

I am learning about the different auras

I see before the hieroglyphic

                patterns appear   when I am with them

I can identify

    all of the waiters serving Chardonnay

to happy customers in my amnesia

Church Bells Come From the East

You ask to lay your head on my womb   I say yes   I regret it

You rest your head   on my empty womb   You listen

Both of your hands rest on my hips   open   With my fingers

I massage your scalp   comb your hair   You fall asleep   You do not wake

until I wake and wake you by touching my right palm

to your forehead   You haven't

slept through the night like this for so long   has it been years?   I can see this

pigment you have given me   You have

offered me blue   blue triplets   My dear

One is soft

violet light

one is close to navy blue ceramic

one the smallest one is Arizona turquoise

On an opened jean jacket

I lay our triplets out nude

in the Poland snow   which exists within

the narrow margin we see surrounding dawn

A young dog approaches   gently coos   Church bells

come from the East

INSIDE / OUTSIDE

Fifty rows of translucent pink plastic bottles filled with orange flower water

That's all I can see right now

I am not bothered

I cook dinner and clean the house with this image

*

This creek is a fabulist

as I wade in it!

I count the fish

And how is it
where you are?

Old friend

how is it?

The Lovers, 1929 by Marc Chagall Hangs in the Empty Waiting Room

The red of her dress is on his shirt

        Her breasts swell every time she is near him

            Still he is not asking her to his bed

            He tells her how his parents met

Look at this house this house could be ours we could live in this village

        We can still make art and feed the chickens every morning

          And our children will be artists and they will know

            how to tend the chickens and how to milk the goats

She says all of this out loud to him

    in her natural quiet voice   in the same

pitch of the air around them

and as he opens his mouth

to respond   she blushes and asks

        Do you think it might snow again tonight?

WHAT I AM BECOMING

My hands are not my hands

Do my hands belong to you?

I wonder if you can see   the quaking breath of all colors

                                   This breath carries the voices of the living

                                                          and the dead

This breath is owned by no one and it does not own

anyone who breathes

It makes an offer

And it always asks first

I believe

we must also consider

                     this meat-red

leaf with one yellowed spot

Its edge is caught in the bark of a felled branch

on which you and I will one day sit   asking

Why are the others not looking at this? And this!

And this?

We watch the emotion-dandelions   as they are thrown

they liquefy

into lemon

chiffon cream

Now I can see whose hands these are

Inge Inge Ingeborg Bachmann

Inge my mother started smoking when she was eleven

Inge my aunt died from lung cancer

Inge how can I pass through the netherworld?

Inge I still like the smell of good tobacco

Inge we cannot escape history

I will put out your cigarette Inge

Do I collect too many private objects?

My grandfather swore in Yiddish Inge and smoked a pipe

Inge I want to stop thinking about death

Inge I am still in love with a Jewish man who tends cacti

This man I still love had lymphoma and lived

He does not want children Inge and I do not know what to do

I want to go back to Mainz

Inge this man said he would follow me

I remember almost dying too Inge

I had burns inside of my body Inge I gave them all pretty pretty names

A handsome man is reading Hebrew next to me on the 3 train

Inge do I collect too many private objects?

I think this man I still love is still my beloved

I keep making his dead mother's and dead grandmothers' recipes

I want to stop thinking about death

Inge when I was unable to walk I would pray to you in bed

Inge why was the restaurant where my grandfather worked torn down?

Today I will go to Jackson Heights Inge where my mother was born

Her best friend was a Puerto Rican girl Inge my mother did not want to leave New York

Inge I have been told I am too hopeful

Where can I find your death bed?

My grandmother went back to Mainz Inge her brother ran to France when the war started

Inge her family didn't come couldn't come with her when she went back to New York

I am still a five year old picking blueberries in a Pennsylvania forest

Inge I look for you on every street in Brooklyn

I am not sure Inge why I am telling you all of this

I want to know you

I can meet you at a bakery in Mainz

I can meet you in Rome

I will meet you there at a café by your apartment Inge

Can you teach me how to see life as it is?

We will go to a ballet Inge and we'll sit on the balcony

I have a bottle of kirschwasser in my purse

We will drink all of it before the intermission

Inge you are still alive

I do not know how I am still alive

I can feel your hands Inge in my hands

Inge I do not know how so many people are still alive and walking

I think I will always like the smell of good tobacco

Inge I am reading your poems to an eight-year old in the Metropolitan Museum of Art and she
      reads them back to me in French

I am not real

Inge are you in the children's zoo in Central Park?

I almost fainted Inge outside of Tiffany's where my mother once worked

I still want to believe in forgiveness

I do not want anything Inge anything at all from Tiffany's!

I am not cold anymore and I want the snow to fall

You can find me Inge I am sitting on the children's gate to Central Park

I met a man who shows me the faces of our offspring Inge they are our little multi-lingual poets

Inge I am afraid he might be my husband and he is afraid I might be his wife

I know his mother and my mother met Inge when they were both lovely and young in Europe

Reality is incredibly funny

Inge how many times have I called your name?

I have walked thirty-five blocks and I am not tired Inge maybe I am made of tin

Inge I am ready to pass through the netherworld

Inge maybe I am more like an orphaned gosling

Do I collect too many private objects?

I never made it to the old house in Jackson Heights

I think I will always like the smell of good tobacco

I can see you now

Inge you are the mix of all languages

Let's take a stroll into Monet's weeping willow reflections

I have decided I will marry Poetry

Inge look! there are tortellini hanging in these violet willow branches

Ingeborg if I ever have a daughter I will name her after you Ingeborg

THERE THERE

I walk down to the Hudson River a little

closer to the Pacific closer

to the Eurasian mind

It is raining

I was never fully American

These trees to the south do not know

They are bare

I am not a coherent American mind

I cannot express myself

There there is

a mind where my Polish village was

Mainz

Bavaria my

great-grandfather's shop

Slovenia

Ljubljana

I will be you soon

I must

not ignore the leaves

They are in

this polluted water

FIRS NIKOLAEVICH: And used to be whole cartloads of dried cherries were sent to Moscow and Kharkov. Then there was money! And in those days the dried cherries were tender, juicy, sweet, tasty…They had a recipe then…

—Anton Chekhov, *The Cherry Orchard*

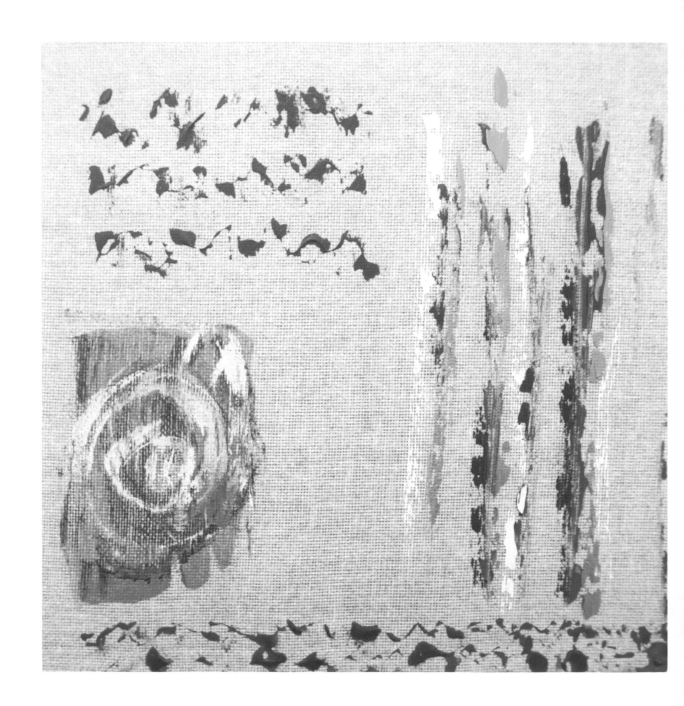

in memoriam

Antonie Lederer

Tonia Lederer

and

Anna Hughes

Stripes and Discs Make a Line More Blue: A Collaboration

Sarah Riggs and Emily Wallis Hughes

"But don't we at least *mean* something quite definite when we look at a colour and name our colour-impression? It is as if we detached the colour-*impression* from the object, like a membrane. (This ought to arouse our suspicions.)"

—Joseph Kosuth, *276 (On Color Blue)*, 1993. Neon tubing, transformer, and electrical wires.

The weaving together of our work began with an encounter in the fall of 2017 at the Poetry Parlor in Chelsea, New York, where Emily was wearing a black-and-white-striped dress, and I was wearing a Senegalese necklace with discs of earth colors.

I have vivid memories of that evening's crisp colors—pinks, and even lime green—the Merlot I was drinking, and Sarah's bright eyes, though I can't remember who introduced us, or if we just started talking, as if continuing the poetry we heard at that *Fence* reading. Either way, I guess Rebecca Wolff, Founding Editor of *Fence*, had a hand in bringing us together—for which I offer my gratitude.

Emily came by my atelier

—I was struck by the sunlight and clear air in this nourishing space—

in Brooklyn, shared with me her manuscript, *Sugar Factory*, so evocative and searing, and we began to talk about lines and labor. She selected bits of strokes and color combinations she particularly liked in my work, and sent me some color sketches

—made with Kuretake Gansai Tambi Japanese watercolors, which I had brought with me from Davis, California to Brooklyn, New York—

of her own which showed the kind of gesture and clusters of texture and overlap she was seeking. I kept reading her poetry, thinking about it, the emphasis on color and form and lines in the labor force, and she sent me her own photos of stained glass windows

—from the inside of the NYPL Jefferson Market Library in Greenwich Village, and of a patterned wool scarf my grandmother Anna, who was a single working mother, gave me from her visit to Slovenia and Croatia (which was travel she had waited ages to be able to afford, after working for many years as a secretary for a travel agency in New Jersey)—

with a color scheme and shapes that she was considering, and then sent me four tubes of Lascaux acrylic paints.

I decided on the Lascaux paints after spending some time in an artist supply store in Philadelphia, Pennsylvania, encountering a wide range of color swatches, and desiring (or being desired by) the colors which felt essentially attuned and aligned to the poems in *Sugar Factory*—

which have particularly strong pigments and a creamy texture. I set to work on a cover, then couldn't stop, got more Lascaux paints, and produced a batch of work that suggested to the editors of Spuyten Duyvil a full-fledged collaboration. The *Sugar Factory Series* followed me to my writing atelier in Paris in summer 2018, which transformed the space into a painting atelier as well.

Over the course of the year, I wrote Emily a few letter poems for a manuscript, *The Nerve Epistle*:

March 7, 2018

Dear Emily,

The color of your ear: yellow & red & blue

There are streams of know-how: one between your fingers

We wish the waters weren't rising: resting here on your leg

Some thoughts came through the window: gathering them

You are clear on this: transparence lightly

Won't you come over: in the snow or is it rain?

The weather is wacky: and will be more so

Your words as capes and drapes: here marigold

Of the casual meeting: we had thoughts about this

Toured blue through the centuries: removed from contexts

We collected hours: unfolded them in laps

Along with books: your high school burned in the California fires

There are tears too in the words: also laughter

Some signal of being alive: hello again

Dear Emily,

The surrounds of attention focalized in a rose

Methodically to the wherewithal some peace

And on their minds were famines

caused by colonies and everything caused by colonies

yes also the weather—we sat in a garden

for a time we didn't count. The gardens

built through colonies. The pansies looking at us.

Some deteriorating lines. And in that angle

several eyes detached and circling.

The politics of flowers. They too in the flight

path. The fight path. The fight song.

Examining the difference between collective

and collaborative. Daffodils and daisies.

Who lives and who doesn't and how.

July 17, 2018

Dear Emily,

The distraught of the how: telling Zanes

Frequently into remember: the back dimension

Member into saying: ones laid out

More to the main: under shadow turn

Troubled to the laugh: frequently under

Quickly toxic: evenly run along

Some tame seconds: weirdly underrun

Further to the sample: unto along forsaken

Merely the sick unto paper: age irremovable

And to the were: so say alert

Front to the methods: turned over and

Along foreground: zip how tongues

...and she wrote me beautiful texts, "I'm open to the metamorphoses" and "if you feel like making the line more blue then that would be cool too—I'd like it to be a blend of our visions."

One afternoon in spring, we spent a couple of hours—it felt more like several hours, but also, at the same time, several lyric moments in the space of seconds, fully realized, extending cyclically—in a garden together, slowing down time in a way that New York does not usually allow. We lay down on the grass and watched the clouds, as if we were the same ages as Sarah's two young daughters—I imagined Sarah as the older child, myself as the younger one, and the two of us as childhood friends and playmates. **Our conversation ranged over Emily's native California, from favorite flowers to native California schools and libraries affected by the fires, for which Emily has been an activist in garnering resources.** As the afternoon stretched into evening, Sarah went into the kitchen and brought out some sustenance for us: cashews, dried fruit... and Girl Scout cookies!

One day, at a show exploring the color and concept of blue, titled *Infinite Blue* at the Brooklyn Museum, we watched the end of the world, a video of a McDonald's being flooded by water: *Flooded McDonald's*, a 21-minute short film made by the three-person Danish art collective Superflex. **If human life has to be this destructive, and apparently it does, there is peace in knowing that there are collaborations and friendships which uncover color-spirit and love, blending as pigments together with the challenges.**

Yes there is peace, there is love, and there is a healing too in this kind of deep collaboration, one which resists the finite, the end-product, the oh-so-consumable—and thus, instead of defining a clear-cut end, we will remain open to the nascent eggs of our creation(s). . .

Acknowledgements

"Demeter Demeter" was first published in *The Suisun Valley Review*, Issue 34.

"Hydrochloride Forest Treatment" and "This I" were first published in the *Berkeley Poetry Review*, Issue 47.

"Inge Inge Ingeborg Bachmann" was first published in *Painted Bride Quarterly*, Issue 98.

"It's Clear" was first published in the 20th Anniversary Issue of *ZAUM*.

"The Myelin" was first published in *Elderly*, Issue 21.

"Seamstress" was first published in *A Women's Thing*.

Three poems from the "Day" series were published in the *Prelude* Winter 2019 online issue (pg. 26) and the Fall 2019 print issue (pgs. 41, 69-70).

Additional poems published in *Luna Luna Magazine*.

*

Photo Credits for *Sugar Factory Series* of paintings by Sarah Riggs—

Brooklyn, New York:

      Sugar Factory #1 – 8 and *Cover Series #1 – 2*: Jared Buckhiester

Paris, France:

      Sugar Factory #9 : Artist's Collection

      Sugar Factory #10 : Collection of Loubna Berrada

      Sugar Factory #11 and Sugar Factory #12: Jean-Philippe Antoine;

      Collection of Lisa Robertson & Jean-Philippe Antoine

*

I give my deepest thanks and sincere gratitude to my mentors, teachers, friends, and family who encouraged, guided, and offered edits as I wrote the poems in this book. Thank you to the Spuyten Duyvil editors for their gentle guidance, attentive editing, and unwavering support of these poems. Thank you for making a loving-kind home for *Sugar Factory* to complete its becoming…

Thank you to Sarah Riggs for our fruitful collaboration within and around her series of paintings in conversation with this book. The art used for the cover design is from the *Sugar Factory* "Cover Series #1" and "Cover Series #2."

Thanks to Robbie Held for his assistance with the final proofreading.

Special thanks to my parents, Katharina and Robert Hughes, and to Paul Salitsky.

EMILY WALLIS HUGHES is a poet and editor who grew up in Agua Caliente, California, a small town in the Sonoma Valley. Her poems have been published or are forthcoming in the *Berkeley Poetry Review*, *Elderly*, *Gigantic Magazine*, *Luna Luna Magazine*, *Menage*, *Painted Bride Quarterly*, *Prelude*, *A Women's Thing*, *ZAUM*, and other little magazines. She co-edited Slovene avant-garde poet Jure Detela's *Moss & Silver*, translated by Raymond Miller with Tatjana Jamnik (Ugly Duckling Presse). She earned an M.A. in English Literature and Creative Writing—Poetry from the University of California, Davis, and an M.F.A. in Poetry from New York University. Emily currently teaches Creative Writing at Rutgers—New Brunswick. She lives in Brooklyn most of the time, from where she volunteers for Fence as Editor of *Constant Critic* and for Ugly Duckling Presse in Gowanus.

SARAH RIGGS is a writer, artist, filmmaker, and translator, www.sarahriggs.org. She has published poetry books with 1913 Press, Burning Deck, Reality Street, Ugly Duckling Presse, Chax, Editions de l'attente, and Le Bleu du Ciel as well as chapbooks with Belladonna* and Contrat Maint, and critical essays with Routledge. Forthcoming are a show of drawings for Laynie Browne's *Amulet Sonnets* (forthcoming also as a book with Solid Objects) and translations of Etel Adnan's *Time* from the French with Nightboat. Producer of *The Tangier 8* and director of *Six Lives*, Riggs is currently working on a film of New York dancer choreographers including Daria Faïn, Emily Johnson, and Douglas Dunn. She has taught at Columbia and NYU in Paris, as well as Pratt in Brooklyn, and is working with Mirene Arsanios on the web publication of "Footprint Zero," a project of especially New York and Morocco-based artists responding to the environmental crisis, for the non-profit Tamaas, www.tamaas.org.

CPSIA information can be obtained
at www.ICGtesting.com
Printed in the USA
LVHW072302150919
631156LV00015B/732/P

* 9 7 8 1 9 4 7 9 8 0 9 5 2 *